Jacine Star

GW00500113

How to Talk to your Dog

Building a Strong Connection through Effective Connection

INTRODUCTION

CHAPTER 1

LAYING A SOLID COMMUNICATION FOUNDATION
Introduction
Bonding and Trust:
Establishing Consistency:
Positive Reinforcement Training:
Establishing Communication:
FEEDING CUES: HOW TO RECOGNIZE WHEN YOUR DOG IS HUNGRY

CHAPTER 2

IMPROVING COMMUNICATION WITH BODY LANGUAGE
Maintain a Calm and Relaxed Body Posture:
Eye Contact and Facial Expressions:
Body Language and Control:
Physical signals to Reinforce communications:
Observe and Respond to Your Dog's Body Language:
1. PAYING ATTENTION TO YOUR DOG'S BODY LANGUAGE
Position of the tail:
Ear Positioning:
Body Posture:
Facial Expressions:
2. USING BODY LANGUAGE
Relaxed and Open Posture:
Establishing adequate eye contact can communicate trust and confidence:
Facial Expressions:
Hand Gestures:
Movement and Energy:
Use Appropriate Space:
Timing and Consistency
3: USING VISUAL CUES TO REINFORCE MESSAGES
Pairing Verbal Orders with Visual Cues:
Consistency and repetition
Positive reinforcement:
Gradual Removal of Visual Cues:
Individualize Visual signals:
HOW TO TELL YOUR DOG IS SICK
Changes in Eating or Drinking Habits
Lethargy or Lack of Energy
Changes in Bathroom Habits
Vomiting or Diarrhea
Coughing, wheezing, heavy panting, or trouble breathing
Changes in Coat or Skin

Behavioral Changes
Weight Gain or Loss
Persistent Pain or Discomfort
WHEN DOES YOUR DOG NEED TO BE BATHED?
Stench
Dirty or Matted Coat
Excessive oiliness or greasiness
Itchy or Irritated Skin
Fleas or ticks that are visible
Mats and Tangles
Stains or discoloration
Seasonal Considerations

CHAPTER 3

ADAPTING COMMUNICATION TO YOUR DOG'S SPECIFIC NEEDS
Understanding Your Dog's Personality
Recognizing Sensitivities
Changing Training Approaches
Establishing Consistency
Patience and Flexibility
Obtaining Professional Help
1. EXPAND ON BREED-SPECIFIC CHARACTERISTICS
Check Breed Standards
Talk to Breed Experts
Consider Genetic Testing
Individual Variations
Training and Exercise Routines
Look for Breed-Specific Communities
2. EXPAND ON INDIVIDUAL CHOICE ADAPTATION
Pay special attention to your dog's body language, vocalizations, and reactions to various situations
Customize Your Dog's Reward and Motivation
Respect Personal Space
Adjust Training Methods
Determine Preferred Communication Indications
Enrichment and Activities
Be patient and flexible
3. EXTENSIVE CONSTRUCTION ON THE FOUNDATION
Reinforce Basic Commands
Expand Vocabulary
Establish Communication Signals
Maintain a Positive Tone and Body Language
Active Listening
Seek Professional Training

CONCLUSION

Introduction

"How to Talk to Your Dog*: Building a Strong Connection Through Effective Communication"*

Welcome to "How to Talk to Your Dog: Building a Strong Connection Through Effective Communication." This book is intended to be an all-inclusive guide to understanding and strengthening your communication with your loving canine companion. Dogs have been our trusty companions for thousands of years, and we may deepen our bond, develop our relationship, and form a happy partnership via good communication.

As dog owners, we frequently wish we could have meaningful conversations with our canine companions. While dogs may not grasp our language as well as we do, they do have their ways of communicating with us. This book will provide you with the information and strategies to bridge the communication gap, allowing you to better understand your dog's needs, desires, and feelings.

The first chapter, "Building a Strong Foundation for Communication," will look at the fundamental concepts of effective communication. You will learn how to set the groundwork for a solid connection with your dog, from establishing trust and respect to creating a pleasant learning environment. You will also learn to know when your dog is likely to be hungry and recognize the cues

The second chapter, "Enhancing Communication Through Body Language," dives into nonverbal communication. Dogs communicate primarily through body language, and you can read their messages and respond correctly by learning their clues (which may include feeding cues and bathing cues), signals, and gestures. We will look at both observing your dog's body language and using your body language to effectively transmit signals.

"Tailoring" Chapter 3 "Communication to Your Dog's Needs" goes into each dog's uniqueness. Dogs, like people, have distinct personalities, interests, and communication methods. This chapter will walk you through the process of tailoring your communication to your dog's individual needs, from analyzing breed-specific qualities to recognizing sensitivities and altering training methods accordingly.

This book contains practical advice, real-life examples, and step-by-step directions to help you create a stronger bond and effective communication with your dog. Whether you are a first-time dog owner or have had dogs in your life for years, there is always room to enhance your communication skills and strengthen your bond with your canine companion.

Keep in mind that good communication is a two-way street. By observing and listening to your dog, you can develop a language of understanding and a lifelong bond by listening to their indications and altering your approach. Prepare to start on an adventure of discovery, comprehension, and meaningful communication with your dog. Let's get started!

Chapter 1

Laying a Solid Communication Foundation

Introduction

Communication is essential for developing a strong and lasting bond with your dog. By laying a solid communication foundation, you will be able to better understand your dog's needs, feelings, and desires, as well as effectively transmit your messages to them. In this chapter, we'll go over the actions you need to take to set the stage for successful communication with your pet.

Understanding Canine Communication: To effectively interact with your dog, you must first understand how dogs communicate with one another. Dogs express their feelings and intentions through a combination of body language, vocalizations, and scent. To effectively read your dog's emotions, study the numerous postures, facial expressions, and tail positions. This information will enable you to reply correctly and develop a rapport.

Bonding and Trust: Effective communication requires a solid link between you and your dog. Spend meaningful time with your dog doing activities he enjoys, such as walks, play sessions, and training. Positive experiences build trust and improve your connection. To encourage your dog's desired behaviors, use positive reinforcement strategies such as treats, praise, and caressing. Your dog will be more likely to listen and respond to your communication efforts if you create pleasant connections with your presence and conversations.

Establishing Consistency: When speaking with your dog, consistency is essential. Routines and clear expectations are important to dogs. Use consistent cues and directions for certain actions, and make sure that everyone in the family speaks and gestures in the same way. Dogs learn through consistent communication helping them grasp what you anticipate from them through repetition. This consistency extends to your actions and reactions. Maintain a cool and composed demeanor to provide a stable and dependable presence on which your dog may rely.

Positive Reinforcement Training: Positive reinforcement training is an excellent way to communicate with and modify your dog's behavior. Reward your dog for good behavior with treats, praise, or toys. Your dog will learn to repeat certain behaviors if you associate pleasant results with them. This strategy fosters mutual understanding and improves communication between you and your dog.

Establishing Communication: Communication is a two-way street that requires active listening and observation. Pay close attention to your dog's indications and behaviors. Take note of their body language, vocalizations, and overall insights into their wants and feelings. Keep an eye out for minor changes in their behavior that may suggest discomfort, anxiety, or joy. You can effectively address your dog's problems and provide the appropriate support if you are alert and responsive.

To build a firm foundation of communication with your dog, you must first understand their natural communication styles, then create trust, and consistency, and use positive reinforcement training approaches. You set the foundations for a healthy and gratifying connection with your furry companion by devoting time and effort to establishing this foundation. The following chapter will go into greater detail on improving communication through body language.

Feeding Cues: How to Recognize When Your Dog is Hungry

Recognizing your dog's eating cues is a crucial part of understanding their needs and feeding them at the appropriate times. Dogs, like people, have their unique ways of expressing hunger. You may learn to determine when your dog is hungry by paying attention to their **habits and cues.**

Here are some frequent warning signs to look out for:

Increased Alertness: Dogs may become more alert and attentive when they are hungry. They may begin to scan their surroundings, paying particular attention to the location where their food is generally provided.

- Pacing and restlessness: Pacing and restlessness are prominent indications of hunger in dogs. If your dog begins to move around more, it could be an indication that they are hungry.

- Whining or Vocalization: When dogs are hungry, they may vocalize or whine. This could be their way of connecting with you. If your dog begins to whine or make more noise than usual, it could be an indication that they are hungry.

- Increased salivation: When dogs are anticipating food, they may salivate more than usual. In anticipation of a meal, you may observe them licking their lips or drooling. This increased salivation could be a sign that your dog is hungry. When dogs are hungry, they may exhibit behaviors connected with food searching... they may sniff about the kitchen or food storage area, paw at their food bowl, or even attempt to open cupboards or containers containing their food.

- Attention to Food-Related Activities: If your dog becomes overly interested in food-related activities, such as watching you prepare meals, following you into the kitchen, or showing attention when food is served to others, it could be an indication that they are hungry themselves.

- Reduced Interest in Other Activities: When a dog is hungry, he or she may lose interest in playing, interacting, or engaging in normal activities. Instead, they may concentrate on finding food or anticipating their next meal.

- It is crucial to remember that individual dogs may exhibit slightly different behaviors, and some dogs' hunger signals may be more subtle than others. As a result, it's critical to study your dog's behavior and become acquainted with its indications over time.

Recognizing your dog's feeding cues and responding to their need promptly can guarantee that they get the nutrition they require. Maintaining their general health and well-being will be aided by establishing a regular meal schedule and offering suitable portion sizes based on their age, size, and dietary requirements.

Remember, if you are concerned about your dog's appetite or feeding habits, seek professional advice from your veterinarian.

[?]

[?]

Chapter 2

Improving Communication with Body Language

Body language is important in how dogs communicate with one another and with humans. You may improve your communication with your dog, build your bond, and foster mutual understanding by knowing and skillfully employing body language. This chapter will look at ways to improve communication through body language.

Learn Canine Body Language: Become acquainted with the many body language signals used by dogs to describe their emotions and intentions. Examine your dog's posture, tail position, ear positioning, facial expressions, and overall body tension. A comfortable body with a wagging tail, for example, denotes enjoyment and friendliness, whereas a stiff body with a tucked tail denotes fear or discomfort. Understanding these signals allows you to respond appropriately and modify your body language.

Maintain a Calm and Relaxed Body Posture: Maintain a calm and relaxed body posture when communicating with your dog. Avoid abrupt or jerky movements, which might shock or intimidate your dog. Instead, maintain a relaxed posture and open body language while standing tall. This encourages your dog to approach you and builds trust and comfort. If your dog is worried or scared, squat or sit to appear less intimidating and more friendly.

Eye Contact and Facial Expressions: Eye contact and facial expressions are effective instruments for communication. Direct eye contact, especially with shy or frightened dogs, might be viewed as a challenge or threat. Instead, soften your look and slightly avert your glance to convey a non-threatening presence. Smiling and gentle facial gestures can also assist to establish a positive environment and relax your dog. Pay attention to how your dog reacts to your facial expressions and make adjustments as needed.

Body Language and Control: When walking your dog on a leash, body language and control is essential for efficient communication. Maintain a loose grasp on the leash and avoid tugging or strain. Walk boldly and purposefully to show your dog that you are in command. If your dog pulls or exhibits undesirable behavior, shift their attention quietly and reward them for walking beside you.

Physical signals to Reinforce communications: In addition to verbal directives, use physical signals to reinforce your communications. Combine a hand, for orders such as "sit" or "stay," use a verbal command to signal. Make constant, precise gestures that your dog will comprehend. Your dog will eventually link the visual cues with the desired behaviors, making communication easier.

Observe and Respond to Your Dog's Body Language: It's crucial to pay attention to your dog's body language as well as your own when communicating with them. Observe how your dog reacts to your cues and make necessary adjustments. If your dog exhibits signs of discomfort or tension, such as lip licking, yawning, or looking away, rethink your approach and provide additional support or space as needed.

Improving communication through body language allows you to better understand and respond to the needs and emotions of your dog, you can establish a more profound and effective line of communication with your dog by learning and using canine body language, maintaining a calm and relaxed posture, using appropriate eye contact and facial expressions, mastering leash, and body control, reinforcing messages with body cues, and actively observing your dog's body language. The following chapter will go through how to tailor communication to your dog's specific needs.

1. Paying attention to your dog's body language

Body language is an important part of efficient communication with your dog. Dogs largely communicate via their body postures, facial expressions, and movements. You can acquire vital insights into your dog's emotions, intentions, and overall well-being by carefully studying these signals. When observing your dog's body language, keep the following points in mind:

Position of the tail: The location and movement of your dog's tail might convey important indications about his mental state. A wagging tail denotes happiness or joy, but a tucked tail denotes fear or concern. A stiffly held or lifted tail may be an indication of vigilance or dominance. Take note of the wag's pace and intensity, as they can signify varying levels of arousal.

Ear Positioning: The location and movement of your dog's ears might convey vital information. Forward-facing ears typically suggest focus or curiosity. Ears pressed against the head may indicate fear or submission. Erect ears may signal attentiveness or confidence. Understanding your dog's ear locations will allow you to judge their level of comfort in various scenarios.

Body Posture: The entire body posture of your dog is a crucial predictor of their emotional state. A flexible and relaxed body conveys contentment, whereas a stiff and rigid body denotes worry or anxiety. Take note of whether your dog is standing tall and firmly or hunched low to the ground since this might reveal information about their confidence level and probable fear or nervousness.

Facial Expressions: Dogs have a wide variety of facial expressions that might convey their feelings. Examine their eyes, brows, mouth, and overall muscle tension in their face. A furrowed brow or narrowed eyes may indicate alertness or possible violence, whereas soft and relaxed facial characteristics often reflect relaxation and enjoyment. Stress or discomfort can also be indicated by yawning, lip licking, or panting.

In addition to body language, vocalizations such as specific messages are sent by barking, snarling, whining, or howling. Different barks or vocalizations might communicate different emotions or intentions, like excitement, fear, warning, or playfulness. You can better comprehend what your dog is attempting to communicate by listening to and recognizing these vocal signals.

Remember to take into account the context and overall consistency of your dog's body language. Depending on the situation or the individual dog, several signs may have varied meanings. It is critical to continuously study your dog's body language throughout the day, noting any patterns or changes. This can assist you in establishing a baseline understanding of their communication style and recognizing when anything is wrong or needs to be addressed.

You can obtain a better understanding of your dog's feelings and needs by paying great attention to their tail position, ear placement, body posture, facial expressions, vocalizations, and the context and consistency of their signals. This comprehension will enable you to respond appropriately, alleviate any problems or discomfort, and deepen your relationship with your canine partner. In the following chapter, we'll look at how to use your body language to improve communication with your dog.

2. Using body language

Communicating with your dog requires you to use your body language successfully. Dogs are extremely sensitive to human body language and can read it to grasp your intentions, feelings, and expectations. Here are some essential ways to improve communication with your dog through body language:

Relaxed and Open Posture: When dealing with your dog, maintain a relaxed and open posture. Standing tall with your shoulders relaxed and your arms crossed can be regarded as a defensive or hostile position. A relaxed posture communicates to your dog that you are approachable and non-threatening, which fosters trust and comfort.

Establishing adequate eye contact can communicate trust and confidence: However, direct and indirect extended eye contact is a challenge or danger. Instead, communicate your attention and intent by making soft and compassionate eye contact. Avoid staring or intense gaze, especially if your dog is being anxious or fearful.

Facial Expressions: Dogs can detect and respond to your facial expressions. To portray enthusiasm and warmth, smile and employ a nice, relaxed look. Avoid scowling or frowning, as these expressions can indicate stress or discontent. Your facial expressions should match the tone of your voice and the emotional condition you wish to portray to your dog.

Hand Gestures: Use hand gestures to supplement vocal commands. Because dogs are visual creatures, using hand signals can help reinforce your messages. Maintain precise, consistent, and deliberate hand motions. Raising your hand with an open palm, for example, can be used to signify a stop or stay, whilst pointing in a certain direction can indicate the desired course or place.

Movement and Energy: Your dog's response might be influenced by your movement and energy level. Move with purpose and confidence, particularly during training sessions or when issuing directions. A calm and forceful demeanor is more likely to elicit a response from a dog. Unusual or frenetic motions can confuse or upset your dog.

Use Appropriate Space: Be mindful of your proximity to your dog, as it might alter their comfort and behavior. If your dog appears nervous, approach them quietly and give them personal space. Respect their boundaries and allow them to come to you if they are apprehensive. Being conscious of your spatial awareness demonstrates to your dog that you understand and value their requirements.

Timing and Consistency: Body language consistency is essential for effective communication. Repetition and consistency are how dogs learn. For certain orders and behaviors, use the same body cues and gestures every time. This helps your dog correlate visual cues with desirable activities, making them easier to understand and respond to.

Remember that every dog is different, and their reactions to your body language may differ. It is critical to monitor and comprehend your dog's unique preferences and sensitivities. Take note of how they react to various bodily cues and adapt your approach accordingly. You may improve your bond with your dog and communicate more successfully on a nonverbal level by employing excellent body language. The following chapter will go through how to tailor communication to your dog's specific needs.

3: Using Visual Cues to Reinforce Messages

Introduction: Using visual signals in addition to vocal directions and body language can improve communication with your dog. Visual cues act as unambiguous signals to reinforce your messages, allowing your dog to understand and respond accordingly. In this chapter, we'll look at how to use visual signals to reinforce your conversation with your pet.

Choosing Visual Cues: When selecting visual cues, consider motions or signs that are unique, consistent, and simple for your dog to understand. As visual clues, simple hand gestures or body movements work well. Raising your hand with an open palm, for example, can indicate "stop" or "stay," whereas pointing can direct your dog's attention to a specific spot. To avoid confusion, use consistent visual cues for each order or conduct.

Pairing Verbal Orders with Visual Cues: Use visual cues in conjunction with verbal orders to effectively reinforce your messaging. Begin by issuing the verbal order and the associated visual cue at the same time. For example, when training your dog to sit, say "sit" while guiding them into the sitting position with a hand signal. During training sessions, repeat this pairing to help your dog identify the visual signal with the desired behavior.

Consistency and repetition: Consistency and repetition are essential when it comes to reinforcing messages with visual clues. During training sessions, practice the visual cues regularly, making sure that the same visual cue is utilized for the same command each time. Repetition assists your dog in understanding and internalizing the link between the visual signal and the desired behavior. Allow your dog plenty of opportunities to practice and learn.

Positive reinforcement: This is essential when employing visual signals, as it is with any type of communication. Reward your dog with food, praise, or play anytime he or she correctly responds to a vocal order that is supported by a visual signal. Positive reinforcement reinforces the link between the visual signal, the behavior, and the

reward, increasing the likelihood that your dog will repeat the desired action in the future.

Gradual Removal of Visual Cues: Once your dog has consistently correlated the visual cues with the desired behaviors, you can gradually remove the visual cues from his environment. Begin by employing visual signals in conjunction with spoken commands, then progressively lessen the intensity or prominence of the visual cue over time. Your dog will eventually respond to the vocal command alone, demonstrating that they have assimilated the link between the command and the behavior.

Individualize Visual signals: Because every dog is different, some may respond better to specific visual signals than others. Pay attention to your dog's reaction and, if necessary, change the visual signals. If your dog is not reacting to a specific visual cue, try a new gesture or hand signal. The idea is to identify visual cues that are simple to understand and significant to your specific dog.

Using visual cues to reinforce messages is a powerful strategy for communicating with your dog. You can develop your relationship with your dog by utilizing clear and consistent visual cues, matching them with vocal orders, employing positive rewards, and gradually fading out the visual cues over time. Remember to tailor the visual clues to your dog's preferences and responses. Visual cues can become an effective element of your communication repertoire with practice and patience.

How to Tell Your Dog Is Sick

Part of effective non-verbal communication is recognizing when your dog is ill, it is critical for his or her health and early veterinarian attention. Because dogs cannot express their displeasure verbally, it is critical to remain watchful and observe changes in their behavior, look, and overall health.

Here are some symptoms that your dog may be sick:

Changes in Eating or Drinking Habits
Loss of appetite, rapid weight loss, increased or decreased thirst, or changes in eating and drinking habits can all be symptoms of sickness. If your dog repeatedly refuses food or drink, it could be a sign of an underlying health problem.

Lethargy or Lack of Energy
If your normally active and enthusiastic dog becomes unusually lethargic, fatigued, or loses interest in activities they normally love, this is a sign of a problem.

When dogs are not feeling well, they may show less excitement for exercise, playfulness, or walks.

Changes in Bathroom Habits

Keep an eye out for any changes in your dog's toilet habits. This includes increased urination frequency or urgency, urination difficulties or discomfort, bloody or discolored urine, diarrhea, constipation, or major changes in stool consistency.

Vomiting or Diarrhea

While occasional vomiting or diarrhea may not signal a significant condition, persistent or recurring bouts should be addressed seriously. Furthermore, if the vomit or diarrhea contains blood or is accompanied by other symptoms, it is critical to seek veterinarian care.

Coughing, wheezing, heavy panting, or trouble breathing

This can all be symptoms of respiratory distress or sickness. The presence of labored or fast breathing, frequent coughing, or blueish gums is cause for concern. Immediately seek veterinary care.

Changes in Coat or Skin

Watch for changes in your dog's skin and coat. Excessive shedding, dryness, flakiness, redness, swelling, lumps, pimples, rashes, hot spots, or any signs of discomfort, itching, or pain are examples of these.

Behavioral Changes

Any apparent changes in your dog's behavior may be a sign of an underlying problem. This can involve unexpected aggression or fearfulness, as well as sudden aggression, heightened irritability, anxiety, restlessness, pacing, bewilderment, and disorientation.

Swelling, redness, discharge, cloudiness, or odd odors from your dog's eyes, ears, or nose can be indicators of infection, injury, or other health issues. A veterinarian should also be consulted if there is severe weeping, squinting, or rubbing of the eyes.

Weight Gain or Loss

Rapid weight loss or increase without a change in diet or exercise might be problematic. Visible changes in physical condition, such as a bulging or bloated abdomen, can potentially be indicators of a health problem.

Persistent Pain or Discomfort

Dogs may express pain or discomfort by vocalization, limping, difficulty getting up or lying down, aversion to being touched or handled, or changes in posture or movement patterns.

It's crucial to realize that these symptoms can differ based on the dog and the underlying disease. It's recommended to visit a veterinarian if you detect any substantial or alarming changes in your dog's behavior, appearance, or overall health. They are capable of making an accurate diagnosis, recommending appropriate treatment, and ensuring your cherished pet's well-being.

When does your dog need to be bathed?

Knowing when your dog needs to be bathed is critical for their hygiene and overall cleanliness. While the frequency of bathing varies depending on breed, coat type, and activity level, there are certain common indications that your dog is due for a bath. Here are some warning indicators to check for:

Stench

If your dog has a visible and persistent stench despite frequent combing and brushing, it may be time for a bath. Dogs' coats can gather dirt, debris, and oils, resulting in an unpleasant odor.

Dirty or Matted Coat

If your dog's coat is dirty, muddy, or stained, it is a strong indication that he is suffering from allergies, a bath is required. Dogs who spend time outside, roll in the grass, or indulge in dirty activities are more likely to require bathing regularly.

Excessive oiliness or greasiness

This in your dog's coat can indicate that it's time for a bath. Some dogs create more oils than others, and these oils can accumulate over time, making their coat appear oily or dull.

Itchy or Irritated Skin

If your dog is scratching, biting, or licking itself excessively, this could be an indication of skin irritation or allergies. A bath can help relieve some of the soreness while also removing allergens or irritants that may be contributing to the condition.

Fleas or ticks that are visible

If you discover fleas or ticks, or other parasites on his coat, he should be bathed with a flea and tick shampoo to help eliminate the infestation.

Mats and Tangles

Mats and tangles in your dog's coat can build over time, particularly in breeds with longer or denser hair. If you detect mats or tangles that are difficult to remove, a bath might help loosen them and make grooming easier.

Stains or discoloration

Stains or discoloration on your dog's coat can be caused by certain substances or environmental factors. Tear stains around the eyes, for example, or stains from urine or feces may require a bath to be effectively removed.

Seasonal Considerations

Your dog's bathing requirements may change depending on the season. As an example, more frequent baths may be required during the spring and summer months, when they may spend more time outside or swimming, to remove allergies, pollen, or chlorine from their coat.

Remember to use dog-specific shampoos and products that are appropriate for your dog's coat type and skin condition. Excessive bathing can deplete your dog's coat of natural oils, causing dryness or skin irritations, so create a balance and don't over-bathe your dog. If you're unsure about the best bathing schedule for your dog, get guidance from your veterinarian or a professional groomer.

Chapter 3

Adapting Communication to Your Dog's Specific Needs

Every dog is unique, having their personality, temperament, and communication style. Understanding and tailoring your approach to your dog's individual needs is critical for effective communication. In this chapter, we'll look at how you can modify your communication style to connect with your dog on a more personal level.

Understanding Your Dog's Personality

Observe and comprehend your dog's personality qualities. Some dogs are more gregarious and sociable than others, and some are shy or reserved. Adapt your communication style to fit their unique characteristics. An outgoing dog, for example, may respond well to vigorous play and effusive praise, whilst a shy dog may require a more delicate and patient approach.

Recognizing Sensitivities

Dogs can be sensitive to specific sounds, movements, or situations. Keep an eye on your dog's behavior and be aware of any triggers that may cause discomfort or anxiety. Avoid or reduce your exposure to certain triggers, and adjust your communication style accordingly. Being aware of your dog's sensitivities demonstrates respect for their boundaries and contributes to a more pleasant and comfortable communication environment.

Changing Training Approaches

Different dogs respond differently to different training approaches. Some dogs may benefit from positive reinforcement training, in which desired behaviors are rewarded, whilst others may require more structure and discipline. Adapt your training techniques to your dog's learning style and motivation. Experiment with several ways and see which ones work best for you and your canine.

Establishing Consistency

Dogs thrive on regularity and consistency. Establish consistent communication patterns for specific activities by employing the same verbal directives, visual signals, and body language. This assists your dog in understanding and anticipating your expectations, which reduces confusion and improves its ability to respond appropriately. Consistency also fosters a sense of security and trust, which strengthens your bond with your dog.

Patience and Flexibility

Because each dog learns at their rate, it's critical to be patient and adaptable in your communication technique. Recognize that, like humans, your dog will have good days and bad days. Allow for pauses and be patient during training sessions. Adapt your communication approach to your dog's energy levels, moods, and receptiveness to new experiences. Flexibility in your approach will aid in the creation of a good and stress-free environment conducive to effective communication.

Obtaining Professional Help

If you're having trouble communicating with your dog or if your dog is exhibiting certain behavioral issues, consider obtaining professional help from a skilled dog trainer or behaviorist. They may evaluate your dog's specific needs and provide tailored guidance and training approaches to increase communication and solve any behavioral difficulties.

Tailoring your communication to your dog's requirements is critical for developing a strong and meaningful bond. You can effectively connect with your dog on an individual level by studying his nature, detecting sensitivities, changing training methods, creating consistency, practicing patience, and obtaining professional help when necessary. This individualized approach not only builds your relationship but also contributes to a happy and pleasurable relationship with your canine buddy.

1. Expand on breed-specific characteristics

Understanding breed-specific characteristics is essential for adapting communication to your dog's needs. Over millennia, many dog breeds have been selectively bred for certain purposes and attributes, resulting in unique traits and behaviors. You can learn about your dog's natural habits, preferences, and communication style by becoming acquainted with breed-specific characteristics. Here are some ways to learn more about breed-specific characteristics:

Consider researching and learning about the traits and history of your dog's breed. Recognize the breed's original function, such as herding, guarding, or hunting. Discover their physical characteristics, energy levels, IQ, and typical disposition. These inherent inclinations and behaviors are made easier with information.

Check Breed Standards

Check the official breed standards established by kennel organizations or breed groups. These guidelines explain the optimal physical and behavioral characteristics of each breed. Understanding the ideal characteristics will help you better understand your dog and how to communicate with them.

Talk to Breed Experts

Contact breeders, trainers, or experienced owners who are knowledgeable about your dog's breed. They can provide useful information about breed-specific features, behaviors, and communication patterns. They may provide recommendations on training approaches, exercise needs, and mental stimulation according to your dog's breed.

Consider Genetic Testing

If you have a mixed-breed dog or are unsure about your dog's breed, consider DNA testing for your dog's breed heritage. Genetic tests can reveal which breeds are present in your dog's genetic makeup. This understanding will allow you to better grasp the breed-specific features they may exhibit and customize your communication accordingly.

Individual Variations

While breed-specific qualities might provide basic knowledge, it's important to remember that individual dogs within a breed can still exhibit differences in behavior and temperament. Not all dogs of the same breed will exhibit the same characteristics. Pay attention to your dog's distinct personality, interests, and communication style, even if they exhibit breed-specific characteristics.

Training and Exercise Routines

Understanding breed-specific features will help you adapt training and exercise routines for your dog. An extremely energetic working breed, for example, a larger companion dog may require more mental and physical stimulus to be content, but a smaller companion breed may have different exercise and training requirements. You can provide appropriate outlets for their energy, mental stimulation, and training exercises that match their natural tendencies by considering breed-specific qualities.

Look for Breed-Specific Communities

Participate in breed-specific communities such as internet forums, social media groups, or local breed clubs. Interacting with other breed owners can bring helpful ideas and experiences. You can share information, ask questions, and learn from those who have direct knowledge of breed-specific characteristics and effective communication tactics.

Understanding breed-specific features is a useful tool for adapting your communication approach to the demands of your dog. By conducting breed research, interviewing breed experts, and contemplating genetic testing, you can expand your understanding of your dog's inherent characteristics and successfully interact with them by noting individual variances, altering training and exercise routines, and discovering breed-specific communities. This comprehension strengthens your bond and allows you to cater to your dog's specific wants and preferences.

2. Expand on individual choice adaptation

Adapting to your dog's unique tastes is essential for efficient communication and the development of a strong bond. Dogs, like humans, have distinct personalities, interests, and communication methods.

Here are some tips for tailoring your communication to your dog's specific preferences:

Pay special attention to your dog's body language, vocalizations, and reactions to various situations

Examine their preferences, dislikes, and levels of comfort in a variety of settings, interactions, and activities. You can better grasp their preferences and alter your communication style by paying attention to their signals.

Customize Your Dog's Reward and Motivation

Determine what motivates and rewards your dog. Some dogs are driven by food, while others may be motivated by praise, play, or toys. Make use of positive approaches with rewards that correspond with your dog's tastes. You can make your dog's training and communication more entertaining and effective by utilizing the correct rewards.

Respect Personal Space

Dogs, like humans, respond differently to physical touch and personal space. Some dogs want close personal contact and affection, while others prefer more space and a little touching. Respect your dog's boundaries and tailor your communication to their needs. Pay attention to their body language to understand whether they want closeness or space.

Adjust Training Methods

Different dogs react differently to training methods. Positive reinforcement strategies may work well for certain dogs, while a more structured approach may be required for others. Take note of how your dog behaves adapting to various training methods and adjusting your strategies accordingly. Be patient and flexible in your search for the training method that best suits your dog's unique learning style and preferences.

Determine Preferred Communication Indications

Each dog may have their own set of cues or indications that they prefer. Experiment with various verbal instructions, hand gestures, and visual signals to see which elicits the appropriate response from your dog. Your dog, for example, may respond better to a specific hand signal for "sit" than to a vocal command. To improve understanding and responsiveness, tailor your communication signals to your dog's preferences.

Enrichment and Activities

Involve your dog in activities and enrichment that correspond to their preferences and interests. Some dogs may benefit from the interaction, others may like peaceful activities such as cuddling or mild walks, while others may favor puzzle toys, agility exercises, or scent work. You may encourage connection and healthy communication by giving activities that your dog enjoys.

Be patient and flexible

Each dog is unique, and it takes time to completely learn their preferences. Allow for trial and error when determining the most successful ways to communicate with your dog. As you learn more about your dog's preferences and requirements, be willing to adapt your communication strategy.

It is critical to adapt to your dog's specific preferences for efficient communication and a solid bond. By studying and listening to your dog, adapting rewards and motivations, respecting their personal space, modifying training tactics, and determining preferred training methods, you can improve your dog's behavior. You can design a communication technique that connects with your dog on a personal level by using communication signals, giving appropriate enrichment and activities, and remaining patient and flexible. This individualized communication promotes trust, understanding, and a strong bond between you and your pet.

3. Extensive construction on the foundation

Building a solid communication foundation with your dog is essential for effective and harmonious relationships. Here are some other methods to expand on that foundation:

Reinforce Basic Commands
Once your dog has learned basic commands like "sit," "stay," "come," and "heel," it is critical to constantly reinforce and practice these commands. Regular practice helps your dog remember the orders and ensures they respond consistently. To encourage and urge your dog to regularly perform these commands, use positive reinforcement tactics, prizes, and praise.

Expand Vocabulary

In addition to fundamental commands, you may broaden your dog's vocabulary by introducing additional words and actions or behaviors. You can teach them words like "fetch," "drop it," and so on. Gradually introduce these terms by utilizing consistent verbal cues and associating them with related actions or behaviors. Your dog will learn to associate these new phrases with specific acts or behaviors with practice and repetition.

Establish Communication Signals

Consider utilizing hand signals or visual clues in addition to spoken commands to improve your communication with your dog. Hand signals can be beneficial in situations where vocal commands may be difficult to understand, such as from a distance or in busy environments. When it comes to establishing communication signals, consistency is essential. Make clear and distinct motions that your dog will recognize and identify with specific acts or behaviors.

Maintain a Positive Tone and Body Language

Dogs are extremely sensitive to human emotions, tone of voice, and body language. Maintaining a positive and calm approach throughout conversations with your dog will improve your communication significantly. When providing directives or praise, use a joyful and encouraging tone of voice. Also, be aware of your body language and facial expressions, since dogs may interpret these signs to determine your intents and feelings.

Active Listening

Active listening is required for effective communication with your dog. Take note of your dog's reactions, body language, and vocalizations. You may better comprehend your dog's needs, feelings, and intentions by carefully listening. This enables you to reply effectively and modify your communication style as needed. Responding to your dog's signals in a timely and compassionate manner fosters trust and enhances your communication link.

Seek Professional Training

If you are experiencing difficulties or wish to enhance your communication skills with your dog, professional training can be beneficial. A professional dog trainer or behaviorist may offer direction, individualized advice, and successful approaches that are tailored to your dog's specific needs. They can also assist in the resolution of any behavioral issues and provide extra ways to build your communication foundation.

To build on the foundation of communication, reinforce basic commands, expand vocabulary, establish communication signals, maintain a positive tone and body language, practice active listening, prioritize consistency and repetition, and seek professional training when necessary. By investing in your connection with your dog regularly, you can deepen the bond, improve comprehension, and develop a happy relationship built on trust and good communication.

Conclusion

Congratulations on finishing "How to Talk to Your Dog: Building a Strong Connection Through Effective Communication." We've covered all you need to know about communicating with your dog, from laying a solid foundation to adapting your approach to your dog's specific needs. You have made a huge step toward creating a peaceful and fulfilling connection with your furry buddy by investing time and effort in studying your dog's language and modifying your communication style.

Remember that communicating effectively with your dog is an ongoing practice. Understanding and connecting with your canine friend involves time, consistency, and a real desire. As you continue your trip, remember how important it is to observe your dog's body language while using your body language successfully, as well as identifying your dog's unique characteristics and preferences.

You may foster a bond based on trust, understanding, and mutual respect by keeping a positive and polite approach, actively listening to your dog's needs, and changing your training approaches. The benefits of excellent communication extend beyond just obedience; they include a strong bond, improved behavior, and a happy, well-adjusted dog.

Remember that each dog is unique, and the tactics and strategies given in this book are intended to be guides only. Take advantage of the opportunity to customize them to your unique dog's needs and personality. Seek professional help when necessary, and continue to learn and grow alongside your pet.

May you have delight as you embark on your road of excellent communication, and language successfully, as well as identifying your dog's unique characteristics and preferences.

You may foster a bond based on trust, understanding, and mutual respect by keeping a positive and polite approach, actively listening to your dog's needs, and changing your training approaches. The benefits of excellent communication extend beyond just obedience; they include a strong bond, improved behavior, and a happy, well-adjusted dog.

Remember that each dog is unique, and the tactics and strategies given in this book are intended to be guides only. Take advantage of the opportunity to customize them to your unique dog's needs and personality. Seek professional help when necessary, and continue to learn and grow alongside your pet.

May you have delight as you embark on your road of excellent communication, joy, and contentment that comes from fully understanding and being understood by your dog. Cherish the times of connection, rejoice in your development, and enjoy the mutual trust and friendship you've developed.

Thank you for selecting "How to Talk to Your Dog: Building a Strong Connection Through Effective Communication" as your reference. May this book be a great resource and source of inspiration for you as you continue your communication journey with your cherished four-legged friend? Here's to a lifetime of adventures, unconditional love, and deep chats with your dog!

Printed in Great Britain
by Amazon

34429445R00031